U0022530

Jenny's mom is very busy.

She works all night and day.

She cooks and cleans and fixes things,

and does it for no pay.

4

"So many things to do today.

The clock says half past two.

I cannot finish everything.

What *am* I going to do?"

5

"First, I have to wash Dad's shirts, and *hang them up to dry.

＊為生字，請對照生字表

I have to *sweep and *mop the rooms."

She said this with a *sigh.

"I also have to clean the toilet
and *iron all the dresses,

then feed the dog and *make the bed,

fix the *drapes and *do the dishes."

But, wait a minute. There's just one thing

before I start the mopping.

Let me think...Ah! Now I know.

I have to do the shopping.

She took her keys and said to Jenny,

"I'm going to the store.

Please be good and watch TV,

and I'll be back at four."

"So many things to do today.

My mother's going crazy.

I should give my mom a hand.

I shouldn't be so lazy."

So she swept her father's favorite shirts,

and washed her mother's bed.

"'Wash the beds and sweep the shirts,'

Yes, I think that's what she said."

With the drapes in the living room

she made a lovely dress.

The dress was really beautiful,

but the drapes were such a *mess.

"I must feed the hungry toilet,"

and she *lifted up the seat.

What did Jenny *place inside?

A can of dog food meat!

She hung up the dishes

and ironed the floor.

Then she mopped the poor dog,
who ran to the door.

Her mother came home.

She was back from the store.

When she saw the big mess,

she fell on the floor.

She looked at the *swept shirts
and she looked at her bed.

She looked at the drapes then
put her hands on her head.

28

"What happened here, Jenny?

Oh! What did you do?

Our dream home's a *disaster.

It's a *nightmare come true!"

Jenny ran behind the sofa.

She was trying to hide.

Jenny's mom started laughing—

she saw the funny side.

"Let's clean up together.

I'll show you how it's done.

Housework can be good for you.

It's exercise and it's fun!"

"Now we've finally finished.

Oh, look! It's half past ten!

I've had such a great time, Mom.

Can we do it all again?"

生字表

（詞性以縮寫表示ㄘˊㄒㄧㄥˋㄧˇㄙㄨㄛㄒㄧㄝˇㄅㄧㄠˇㄕˋ：*v.* 動詞ㄉㄨㄥˋㄘˊ，*n.* 名詞ㄇㄧㄥˊㄘˊ）

越幫越忙

p. 2

珍妮的媽非常忙，日夜瑣事一肩扛。
煮飯打掃修水電，全心奉獻不領錢。

p. 5

「今天好多事要辦，現在卻已兩點半。
每件事都做不完，到底我該怎麼辦？」

p. 6～7

「先洗爸爸的襯衫，將它掛起來晾乾，
還要打掃、拖地板。」說著說著便長嘆。

p. 8～9

「廁所要沖洗才行，衣服要全部燙平，
接著餵狗理床單，修理窗簾又洗碗。」

p. 10

「正要拖地板……且慢，有件事情要先辦。
想一想……靈光一閃！還得購物真麻煩。」

p. 13

拿鑰匙交代珍妮:「我要去商店那裡。
看電視不要亂來，媽媽四點才回來。」

p. 15

「今天好多事要忙，媽媽簡直快抓狂。
我應該幫忙分擔，不可以這麼偷懶。」

p. 16

她掃了爸爸襯衫，還洗了媽媽的床。
「『洗床鋪又掃襯衫，』媽應是這麼打算。」

p. 33

珍妮跑到沙發後，躲著拼命在發抖。
媽媽開始笑出來——最後總算能釋懷。

p. 34

「我們一起來整理，怎麼做我來教妳。
做家事對妳有益，好玩又可練身體！」

p. 36

洗衣、熨衣、修東西，到八點才喘口氣。
接著打掃又拖地，直到很晚才休息。

p. 39

「最後總算全做完，看看已經十點半！
媽咪，這樣真好玩，能不能全部重玩？」

- 說說唱唱學韻文答案：

p. 48   you, zoo, too, who, blue

p. 49   gooses, cheeses, roses, boxes

說說唱唱學韻文

這本書是用韻文來說故事，韻文 (rhyme) 的特色是句子的最後一個字會押韻。當兩個字押韻時，它們字尾的發音是類似的（通常包括一個母音和後面的子音）。讓我們跟著下面的練習，一起來學韻文！

① 請聽 CD 的第四首一起唸，找出這段文字的韻腳：

"So many things to do today. The clock says half past two.

I cannot finish everything. What am I going to do?"

這段文字的韻腳是 two, do。接下來跟著 CD 的第五首一起唸出下列這些字，找出與 two, do 押韻的字。

you, zoo, word, day, bee, too, who, blue

請聽 CD 的第六首，找出這段文字的韻腳：

"I also have to clean the toilet and iron all the dresses,
then feed the dog and make the bed, fix the drapes and do the dishes."

這段文字的韻腳是 dresses, dishes；下面空格裡的字和他們押相同的韻，請將這些句子完成，看看珍妮還幫忙做了其他哪些家事。

I also have to go to the barn, and feed the _____.

Then milk the cow in the farm, and add some cream

and make _____.

Finally I have to water the garden, and pick some _____.

Then I'll make them dry, and put them in the _____.

請聽 CD 的第七首，看看你是不是填對了了！

（答案請見第 47 頁）

請先跟著CD第八首一起大聲朗讀這首童謠「一起去桑樹叢 (Here We Go Round the Mulberry Bush)」，然後跟著唱！唱完之後，還有配樂可以讓你自己獨唱哦！

Here We Go Round the Mulberry Bush

Here we go round the mulberry bush,
The mulberry bush, the mulberry bush.
Here we go round the mulberry bush,
So early in the morning.

This is the way we wash our clothes,
We wash our clothes, we wash our clothes.
This is the way we wash our clothes,
So early Monday morning.

This is the way we iron our clothes,
We iron our clothes, we iron our clothes.
This is the way we iron our clothes,
So early Tuesday morning.

This is the way we scrub the floor,

We scrub the floor, we scrub the floor.
This is the way we scrub the floor,
So early Wednesday morning.

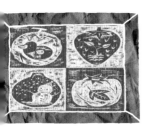

This is the way we mend our clothes,
We mend our clothes, we mend our clothes.
This is the way we mend our clothes,
So early Thursday morning.

This is the way we sweep our house,
We sweep our house, we sweep our house.
This is the way we sweep our house,
So early Friday morning.

This is the way we bake our bread,
We bake our bread, we bake our bread.
This is the way we bake our bread,
So early Saturday morning.

This is the way we go to church,
We go to church, we go to church.
This is the way we go to church,
So early Sunday morning.

1 What Is a Typhoon, Mommy?
媽咪，颱風是什麼？

2 What I Want to Be
我的志願

3 Jenny Helps Do the Housework
越幫越忙

Children's Verses Series
敲敲節奏說韻文系列

Peter Wilds／著　蔡兆倫／繪　王盟雄／譯
精裝／附中英雙語朗讀CD／全套三本
具基礎英文閱讀能力者（國小4～6年級）適讀

珍妮是個古靈精怪的小女孩，在「敲敲節奏說韻文」系列中，她以韻文的方式敘述生活中的趣事，有節奏感的故事聽起來好有趣；她教大家什麼是押韻，還帶小讀者一起唱童謠；她的世界如此豐富，你一定不能錯過！

國家圖書館出版品預行編目資料

Jenny Helps Do the Housework:越幫越忙 / Peter Wilds
著;蔡兆倫繪;王盟雄譯.－－初版二刷.－－臺北市:
三民，2015
    面; 公分.－－(Fun心讀雙語叢書.敲敲節奏說
韻文系列)
中英對照
ISBN 978－957－14－4679－0 (精裝)

1.英國語言－讀本

523.38   95025213

© Jenny Helps Do the Housework
——越幫越忙

著 作 人	Peter Wilds
繪　　者	蔡兆倫
譯　　者	王盟雄
發 行 人	劉振強
著作財產權人	三民書局股份有限公司
發 行 所	三民書局股份有限公司
	地址　臺北市復興北路386號
	電話　(02)25006600
	郵撥帳號　0009998-5
門 市 部	(復北店)臺北市復興北路386號
	(重南店)臺北市重慶南路一段61號
出版日期	初版一刷　2007年1月
	初版二刷　2015年1月
編　　號	S 806951

行政院新聞局登記證局版臺業字第○二○○號

ISBN　978-957-14-4679-0　(精裝)

http://www.sanmin.com.tw　三民網路書店

For You